SCHOLASTIC

LOOK IT UP!

Great Activities for Learning How to Use

REFERENCE BOOKS

by Jennifer O'Neil Plummer

New York • Toronto • London • Auckland • Sydney
Mexico City • New Delhi • Hong Kong • Buenos Aires

Teaching *Resources*

*For my father, who has always
encouraged and supported
my work.*

Cover design by Maria Lilja
Cover photos by Getty Images
Interior design by Maria Lilja
Interior illustrations by Mike Moran and Rebecca Thornburgh (page 10)

ISBN 0-439-49163-0

5 6 7 8 9 10   40   12 11 10 09 08 07

Contents

Introduction

The purpose of this book is to reinforce the importance of traditional research resources. Though other, more sophisticated means for locating information have emerged and enticed many of our young learners, students may not always have access to them. Therefore, it is important to provide all students with the tools and skills necessary to locate and utilize information available in the many traditional sources that still have value in our everyday lives.

How to Use This Book

This book provides straightforward ways to introduce or practice using traditional research resources. The activities enable students to exercise critical-thinking skills as well as practice locating information. They also help promote whole-class and small-group discussion, and serve as spring-boards to the topics you teach.

Prior to beginning the activities, gather as many appropriate resources as possible and create an "Information Corner" in the classroom. Once the resources are in place, try the following introductory activity.

Introductory Activity

Sharing the purpose behind an assigned activity allows students to see the "point" of the exercise and can help increase their motivation and understanding. Initiate a discussion by asking the following questions intended to help students discover the value of using traditional resource materials.

- *Where do we go when we need information?* Students may automatically reply, "Internet!" Encourage them to brainstorm other resources, such as encyclopedia, atlas, and dictionary, as well as telephone book, newspaper, and signs.

- *Are there specific resources for specific types of information?* For example, if you need to get from Pennsylvania to Florida and you want to know which states you will pass through, where would you go to find the answer? Students could respond, "An atlas or a map!"

- *Where would you find the phone number to your favorite pizza shop?* Students may respond, "A phone book!"

- *What types of skills do you need in order to be able to get the information that you seek?* A student might say, "Alphabetizing!" Also, encourage them to think of other skills such as knowing how correctly to spell the word that they are looking up.

Close the discussion by creating a large poster to be displayed in the Information Corner. On the poster, write the names of all the resources that you will be studying. Allow space for a definition of each resource and examples for its use to be filled in after you complete the study of each resource. The poster can then be used as a reference throughout the year.

Meeting National Standards

Many of our national standards indicate that our students need to be able to gather, process, evaluate, and synthesize data from a variety of resources and then communicate their findings in ways that meet their individual needs and purposes. Lessons in this resource provide opportunities for students to learn how to effectively and efficiently acquire information from valuable reference sources so that they can use their new information to further their thinking about and deepen their understanding of a topic or idea. The following are just a few of the key standards that are addressed in activities throughout this resource:

STANDARDS FOR THE ENGLISH LANGUAGE ARTS:

- students conduct research on issues and interests by generating ideas and questions, and by designing problems. They gather, evaluate, and synthesize data from a variety of sources (e.g., print and non-print texts, artifacts, people) to convey their discoveries in ways that suit their purpose and audience.

- students use a variety of technological and information resources (e.g., libraries, databases, computer networks, video) to gather and synthesize information and to accumulate and transmit knowledge.

STANDARDS FOR SOCIAL STUDIES:

- interpret, use, and distinguish various representations of the earth, such as maps, globes, and photographs

- use appropriate resources, data sources, and geographic tools such as atlases, data bases, grid systems, charts, graphs, and maps to generate, manipulate, and interpret information

- locate and distinguish among varying landforms and geographic features, such as mountains, plateaus, islands, and oceans

STANDARDS FOR GEOGRAPHY:

- use maps and other geographic representations, tools, and technologies to acquire, process, and report information

FOR MORE INFORMATION

For more information on national standards visit the Web sites of the following organizations:

- International Reading Association   www.reading.org
- National Council for Geographic Education   www.ncge.org
- National Council of Teachers of English   www.ncte.org
- National Council for the Social Studies   www.ncss.org

Atlas

The Role of the Atlas in Your Classroom

The atlas is a widely used resource in my classroom. In fact, we use it every day for our geography question of the day. Additionally, we use the atlas to identify and learn more about the settings of stories that we read, and the historical and newsworthy locations that we discuss. It is also a helpful resource during distance and measurement activities in math. Becoming familiar with, learning to navigate, and interpreting an atlas can prove to be a valuable tool throughout students' lives.

Lessons

Atlas Comparison

STUDENT OBJECTIVES
• Become familiar with the atlas
• Compare different atlases
• Use critical thinking skills to evaluate each atlas

It is important for students to become familiar with a learning resource before being asked to use it. Provide students with an opportunity to explore their atlas before having to actually navigate through it.

WHAT TO DO

1. Divide students into pairs or groups and allow them to compare different atlases. This will help them to identify the type of information contained in an atlas as well as compare the content of different atlases. Students utilize their critical thinking skills as they evaluate these learning resources to select one that will meet their needs.

2. Distribute copies of the activity sheet for students to complete. You may want to create your own checklist based on your classroom needs.

OLD vs. NEW Tip!

It's a good idea to have atlases that are as up to date as possible. You may want to have on hand an atlas that is very out of date to illustrate this point to students. Show them how some countries have changed names and borders in recent years. For example, what was once Czechoslovakia (one country) is now the Czech Republic and Slovakia (two countries).

MATERIALS
• 2 different atlases for each pair or small group of students
• copies of the Atlas Comparison sheet (page 15) or copies of your own original checklist

Sample questions for creating a checklist:

- *Does the atlas provide information about population?*
- *Does the atlas provide information about climate?*
- *Does the atlas provide information about a country's natural resources?*
- *Does the atlas provide information about a country's special landmarks?*
- *Can you learn about the world's time zones in the atlas?*
- *Is it easy to locate places on the maps?*
- *Are there photographs of actual places included in the atlas?*
- *Is it easy to understand the charts and graphs?*
- *Can you read the longitude and latitude lines easily?*
- *Is the index easy to use?*
- *Are there facts and interesting tidbits of information included in the atlas?*

3. After students have completed the checklists, help extend their thinking by asking them the following questions:

- *If you had to purchases atlases for the class, which atlas would you choose from those that you read? Why?* (Answers might include "The atlas was easy to understand." Or "The pictures and graphs made it more interesting.")

- *Is there information that would be helpful to you that was not included in any of the atlases that you read? What?* (Answers will vary.)

4. Provide an everyday scenario in which an atlas would be a useful tool. (A student might respond, "I might use an atlas when I try to figure out how many miles it is from my house to my grandmother's house." Another student, might say, "I would use an atlas to pick a place that I want to visit some day.")

EXTRA! EXTRA!

Rather than provide a checklist for students, have them look through an atlas to create their own. Help them to identify the different components, content, and information available in an atlas. They can then use their checklists to compare and contrast other atlases to find the one to best suit their needs.

Scavenger Hunt

STUDENT OBJECTIVE

- Locate specific information within an atlas

Once familiar with the contents of an atlas, students will need to practice navigating their way through one. A scavenger hunt is a perfect way to accomplish this. Because atlases can vary in content, you may want to tailor the scavenger hunt to your classroom atlas.

WHAT TO DO

1. Before you begin, familiarize yourself with the atlas that students will be using so that you can ask them to identify information that you are certain is included in it.

2. Distribute copies of the activity sheet for students to complete. It contains questions that could be used with any atlas, regardless of content. Because atlases vary, the answers will depend on the atlas that you are choosing.

MATERIALS
- 1 classroom atlas for each pair or small group of students
- copies of the Scavenger Hunt sheet (page 16)

Sample prompts/questions for creating your own scavenger hunt (the hunt can be based on an entire atlas or specific portions, depending on your needs):

- *Locate the table of contents. On what page is it located?*
- *Use the table of contents. On what page would you find information about _____?*
- *Find the index. On what page is it located? What information is provided in the index?*
- *Use the index. On what page would you find _____?*
- *Find the glossary. Write one word and its definition from the glossary.*
- *Find a picture of _____. On what page is it located?*
- *Find a key that contains information about population. On which page can it be found? What country's population does it describe?*
- *What are the natural resources of _____?*
- *What country is located on page _____?*
- *What type of information is being displayed in the pie graph on page _____?*
- *Which map on page [blank] would be the most helpful to learn about _____?*
- *On the map of Africa, find the longest river.*
- *Locate a map of the United States. List all of the states that border Ohio.*
- *What kind of information does the key on page _____ provide?*

EXTRA! EXTRA!

Rather than turn these questions into a worksheet, use the backs of old maps to write the questions for each student or group. Then, laminate each map and cut the questions into puzzle pieces. Each piece will contain one question in the scavenger hunt. As students answer each question using wipe-off markers, they can work on completing the puzzle to determine the country or city of their map. Once the puzzle is solved, tape it together to view both sides.

Legends and Keys

STUDENT OBJECTIVES

• Understand the purpose of a map legend
• Learn to read a map to identify specific information

Using an atlas, take students on a page-by-page exploration of legends to get a sense of what type of information they include. This activity will help students understand the importance of a legend on a map.

MATERIALS

• 1 classroom atlas for each student or pair of students

WHAT TO DO

1. Ask students to turn to a certain page in their atlas and to cover with their hand the small box in the corner—the legend or key.

2. Then, ask them to share what they think the map is intending to display without giving them an opportunity to look at the legend. For example, see if they can figure out what the stars next to the cities mean, what a dotted line means, or what the other specific icons labeling the map mean.

3. Next, allow them to remove their hands to use the legend to understand the map. Discuss the importance of a legend, what kind of information it contains, and how legends can vary from map to map depending upon the purpose of the map.

4. Continue through the pages until students grasp a legend's purpose.

5. Create a list on the chalkboard or poster paper that defines a legend and contains examples of the types of information it includes.

EXTRA! EXTRA!

Create your own map without a legend or key. The map can re-create your classroom, the setting of the book that you are currently reading, or a location that you are studying in history or social studies class. Whatever you choose, it should be a place familiar to students and should be filled with less rather than more detail. Provide copies of the map to students. Challenge them to create the legend for the map. It will be interesting to see what each student chooses as icons for the legend. After the legend is created, ask students to include the icons on the map itself.

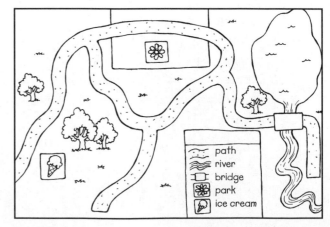

Map Coordinate Bingo

STUDENT OBJECTIVE

• Read longitude and latitude lines to identify specific locations

Provide students with opportunities to use the maps in their atlas by playing Map Coordinate Bingo. You will need to tailor this activity to your classroom atlases.

WHAT TO DO

1. Distribute a blank grid to each student. Note: If you do not wish to include a "free" space, simply cover the icon with a small piece of paper before photocopying.

2. On the chalkboard, list more states than there are squares on the bingo grid. For example, since the reproducible contains 25 squares, you should list the names of approximately 30 states.

3. Ask students to select 24 or 25 of the 30 states (depending on if the "free" space is used). Instruct them to write the name of each state that they choose in a separate square on their bingo grid until it is completely filled.

4. Once everyone's grid is complete, begin calling out coordinate points so that students can locate the correct state, using their classroom atlas.

5. Students need to find the state on their grid. If their grid contains the state, they should mark it with the designated marker. If they did not copy the name of that particular state onto their grid, they cannot mark the grid.

6. Once a student has five markers in a row (vertically, horizontally, or diagonally) they should call out "Bingo!" or whatever term your class chooses.

• copies of the blank bingo grid (page 17) (Note: If creating your own, each grid should contain approximately 25 squares.)

• place markers (10–12 for each student), such as paper squares, popcorn, or any small object

• list of coordinate points (longitude and latitude lines) for each state (Note: This will vary according to the atlas you use.)

• multiple copies of the same atlas for each student or group to use during the game.

Reading Pictures

STUDENT OBJECTIVES
• Learn to read graphs and charts
• Extract information from graphs and charts

They say that a picture is worth a thousand words. Put that to the test! Most atlases contain colorful, detailed illustrations. These illustrations can be photographs, drawings, graphs, or charts. Whatever the illustration, students need to know that these pictorial displays can contain valuable information about a place. Additionally, they need to learn how to access information from these illustrations.

MATERIALS
• sample illustrations from an atlas, including pictures, charts, and graphs

• 1 classroom atlas for each student or pair of students

• notebook paper

WHAT TO DO

1. Introduce the topic by gathering students into a large group. Using the classroom atlas as a reference, discuss the following questions:

• *In what ways do atlases give or display information?* (Students may respond, "Pictures!" "Charts!" "Words!")
• *Why do atlases show some information through pictures or graphs and other information through written text?* (Students may respond that sometimes information is easier to understand if it is drawn rather than written.)

2. Provide examples of different types of illustrations from an atlas. Photographs, charts, and line or bar graphs would be most appropriate.

3. Once they have seen examples, ask students to leaf through their atlases to select a graph or chart in order to study the information that is being displayed.

4. Have students write, in paragraph form, what is being described by the illustration that they have selected. After they have completed writing about their particular illustrations, collect the paragraphs and illustration examples.

5. Divide the class into equal groups. Provide each group with paragraphs and illustrations of charts and graphs, so that no group is reviewing their own work. Ask groups to mix up and then to spread out the illustrations and paragraphs in front of them.

6. Next, ask students to read the paragraphs and then identify the matching illustrations.

7. Once all of the paragraphs are matched with their correct illustrations, gather the whole class for a discussion. Discuss the following questions:

• *Which was easier to understand—the paragraph or the picture illustration?*
• *How do you prefer to view new information?*

• *Is there another way to display the information in a different type of picture form? For example, if the information was displayed in a line graph, could it have been put into a chart or pie graph as well?*

Postcard Greetings

STUDENT OBJECTIVES
• Use knowledge of an atlas to locate a specific location
• Interpret the information being displayed about that location
• Write a piece of text that describes, in some way, the selected location

Once students have become familiar with the atlas and feel comfortable navigating through it, providing them with a larger, more comprehensive assignment will help to assess their abilities before moving on to another learning resource.

WHAT TO DO

1. Ask students to choose a location in the world that interests them. They can be broad (selecting a continent) or they can be more specific (choosing a country or even a city). This depends partly on the atlas they are using.

2. Next, have them use the table of contents and index to locate as much information about their chosen location as possible. Using maps, charts, graphs, and text, students should gather information about their location.

3. Once they have sufficient information, ask them to pretend that they are sending someone a postcard from their location, as if they were actually there. In the postcard, students can include information about where the place is located, its climate, any interesting or special features (physical and historical), or any other relevant facts they can gather.

The activity sheets will help students organize their information and plan their writing. Once they have completed a rough draft of the greeting, students can complete a final draft on the postcard template. Students should illustrate the opposite side of the postcard with points of interest or landmarks from the location about which they have written.

Note: You may want to photocopy the postcard template on card stock so that it is more durable once it is cut. Also, displaying personal postcards from your own collection or those that students have brought can help to guide their creativity.

> ### MATERIALS
> • 1 classroom atlas for each student
> • copies of the Postcard Greetings sheets (pages 18–20)

Atlas Extensions

Once students are familiar with the atlas and how to use it, the atlas can enhance and extend their learning in many ways. The activities below will encourage continued practice with reading an atlas and interpreting the information within it.

Current Events: If you incorporate current events into your curriculum, use the atlas to locate points of interest and learn more about a location that is being described in a news article. Keep a large map in the room that flags all of the places that you have discussed in your current events lessons.

Geography Question of the Day: Every morning when students enter the classroom, provide them with opportunities to jump-start their brain with quick and easy questions. Post a large map in your room. Each day, attach a "question of the day" to the map, or display it on the chalkboard, in a folder or booklet, or on large poster paper. Questions might include:

- *How many states border Canada?*
- *Through which states does the Mississippi River run?*
- *What are the capital cities of the states that border California?*

Investigating Setting: When reading any type of fiction or nonfiction text throughout the day, focus on setting. Ask students to locate the setting in their atlases. Then, gather information from the atlas about the setting to learn more about the role that setting plays in the story they are reading. Additionally, encourage students to consult an atlas when creating their own stories. Ask them to become familiar with a setting they have chosen for their story. To make their stories more realistic and detailed, have them incorporate information that they have gathered from their atlases.

The ABC's of Geography: Have students create colorful, easy-to-read signs that depict each letter in the alphabet. Display these signs in order around the room. As students learn geography terms and identify important locations that relate to the curriculum, have students attach the information to the correct letter of the alphabet. For example, for the letter P, students might affix the words painting, prism, Paris, or Pierre. Displaying the words that you want to become a part of students' everyday vocabulary will be constant reminders and helpful hints.

Name _____ Date _____

Atlas Comparison

What type of information is contained in an atlas? With a partner or small group, use two different atlases to find the answers to the following questions. Circle either yes or no.

Write the name of each atlas under atlas #1 and atlas #2.

	ATLAS #1	ATLAS #2
	_____	_____
1. Are there an index and table of contents?	yes/no	yes/no
2. Are the index and table of contents easy to use?	yes/no	yes/no
3. Are the maps clearly labeled and colorful?	yes/no	yes/no
4. Can you read the longitude and latitude lines easily?	yes/no	yes/no
5. Are there graphs and charts?	yes/no	yes/no
6. Is it easy to understand the graphs and charts?	yes/no	yes/no
7. Is there informational text?	yes/no	yes/no
8. Does the atlas provide information about population?	yes/no	yes/no
9. Does the atlas provide information about climate?	yes/no	yes/no
10. Does the atlas provide information about natural resources?	yes/no	yes/no
11. Does the atlas include information about interesting landmarks?	yes/no	yes/no
12. Can you learn about the world's time zones in the atlas?	yes/no	yes/no
13. Are there photographs of actual places included in the atlas?	yes/no	yes/no
14. Are there facts and interesting tidbits of information included in the atlas?	yes/no	yes/no

Follow-up: Which atlas do you prefer? Why? _____

_____

Name _____ Date _____

Scavenger Hunt

Becoming familiar with the location of specific information in your
atlas will help you to find information more quickly and easily.
Complete this scavenger hunt to learn more about your atlas.

1. Find the table of contents. On what page is it located? _____

2. Use the table of contents. On what page(s) would you find . . .

• information about Australia? _____

• which states border the Great Lakes? _____

• which countries in Europe the Equator passes through? _____

3. Find the index. On what page(s) would you find . . .

• a map of Argentina? _____

• the Seine River? _____

• information about the Himalayan Mountains? _____

4. Find the glossary. Write one word and its definition from the glossary.

_____

5. Find a photograph that shows something specific about a place. What place is being
shown? On what page is the picture? _____

6. Find a chart or graph that shows information about the population of a specific country.
What country's population is being described? On which page can it be found?

_____

7. Find a pie or circle graph. What type of information is being displayed in the graph?
On what page is the graph located? _____

8. What are the natural resources of Brazil? _____

9. Find a map of Africa. Name two rivers located somewhere on the continent.

_____

10. Locate a map of the United States. List all of the states that border California.

_____

© Scholastic Inc. *Look It Up! Great Activities for Learning How to Use Reference Books* page 16

Map Coordinate Bingo

		N W FREE E S		

Name _____ Date _____

Postcard Greetings (Part 1)

Think about a place in the world that you would like to visit one day. This place can be as general as a continent or as specific as a city.

Location: _____

Now that you have selected a place, it is time to learn more about it. Use the table of contents and index of your classroom atlas to find information about your location. You can gather information from pictures, maps, charts, graphs, or the text of the book. Use the space below to record the information that you find.

PAGE NUMBER   INFORMATION GATHERED

_____   _____

                   _____

                   _____

_____   _____

                   _____

                   _____

_____   _____

                   _____

                   _____

_____   _____

                   _____

                   _____

_____   _____

                   _____

Name _____ Date _____

Postcard Greetings (Part 2)

Now that you have collected interesting information about a location, it is time to compile it into a short note to a friend or relative. First, think about postcards that you have written or received. What type of information did they include? How detailed were the descriptions? What was the tone of the greetings?

Write your postcard as if you are visiting the place and actually experiencing what you are sharing. When you write a rough draft, remember to include the following information:

- the name of the person to whom you are writing

- the name of your location

- specific points of interest or landmarks at your location

- a fact or two that describes the physical features of your location

- a closing that includes your name

Name _____ Date _____

Postcard Greetings (Part 3)

Now that you have completed the rough draft of your postcard, it is time to make your final draft. Using the template below, rewrite your postcard greeting. When you have completed your greeting and proofread your work, cut out the postcard and begin your illustration on the back. Create a picture that illustrates your location. Remember to think about postcards that you have received or sent. What type of pictures appeared on them?

Almanac

The Role of the Almanac in Your Classroom

Almanacs can be engaging and intriguing for students. They appeal to students' love of fact-finding and information-gathering of any kind. They allow students to become knowledgeable on topics that aren't necessarily covered in school curricula. Often my students can be overheard leafing through an almanac and calling out bits of information, then racing to the next "cool" topic and reciting that as well. The almanac is often the resource that many students will choose to read when given free time. With the variety of almanacs available today, there is sure to be one to please any taste.

Lessons

Almanac Inquiry

STUDENT OBJECTIVES
• Become familiar with the contents and organization of an almanac
• Define almanac

Before asking students to use an almanac, it is important for them to understand its unique content and organization. Students can then discover an abundance of interesting information.

WHAT TO DO
1. Arrange students into small groups. In each group, every student should have the same almanac. (However, no two groups should have the same almanac.) Be sure to include the current *Farmer's Almanac*, Ben Franklin's *Poor Richard's Almanac*, and any other current grade-appropriate almanacs. As students read through their assigned almanac, they will learn more about its contents.

Tip!

GATHERING ALMANACS

Acquiring a variety of resources for your classroom library can be expensive. Before initiating this unit, or any that incorporates learning resources, it is important to be creative about how to go about gathering enough for classroom instructional use. I have been collecting these resources for years by earning points and free books from student book orders, wish lists from parents, and used book sales.

MATERIALS
• multiple copies of several different almanacs
• chart paper
• markers

2. Provide each small group with the following list of questions that they can answer on large chart paper:

- *What type of information is included in this book?*
- *How is the information organized?*
- *Why would someone use your assigned almanac?*
- *Based on what you have learned so far, what is your definition of an almanac?*

3. Once the groups have answered their questions, have each group present their almanac and their answers to the above questions.

4. Once they each have had an opportunity to present their information, create a class definition for an almanac and then list reasons for using one.

5. Creatively display this information in the "Information Corner" to serve as a visible reminder for students to use an almanac when investigating topics.

Did You Know? Posters

STUDENT OBJECTIVE

- Become familiar with the unique information displayed in an almanac

Providing students with the opportunity to locate and share information that is of interest to them will challenge them to explore their almanac from cover to cover.

MATERIALS

- 1 almanac for each student
- posterboard
- markers or colored pencils

WHAT TO DO

1. Provide each student or small group with an almanac.

2. Ask students to identify topics of interest to them by reading the table of contents or index. For example, students may choose information about the past presidents of the United States or they may look for facts about the currency of other countries. Encourage students to gather information about any topic (as many topics as they choose!).

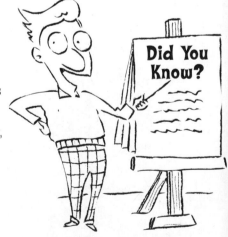

3. Once they have identified the topics that interest them, give them time to gather facts on those topics. Encourage students to record any interesting information that they learn from their almanac. They can record the information on any paper, using it later to create a poster.

4. On posterboard, students can compile and creatively display their facts around the title, "Did You Know?" They may choose to type the facts, cut them out and then paste them on the poster or they may choose to write directly on the poster. No matter what they choose, encourage students to design the poster in a way that is easy to read and eye-catching.

5. Once the posters are complete, invite students to share their posters, displaying them for others to see. Students will be fascinated by the plethora of information contained within an almanac.

Create Your Own Game

STUDENT OBJECTIVE

• Learn to use the table of contents and index to locate information within an almanac

Another way to get students to explore the contents of almanacs is to encourage them to create a game for their classmates to play. This game can take many forms and should be governed only by students' imaginations.

WHAT TO DO

1. Have students identify factual information from the almanac that can be displayed in a game format. Because the object of the game is to get teammates to dig through an almanac to search for answers, the facts should be easily found by using an index or table of contents.

2. Provide materials so that students can create a game board and any necessary pieces.

3. Ask students to transfer their information into a game format. This can replicate the form of any familiar board game. Remind them that the objective of the game will be to have classmates use an almanac to answer the questions in order to move forward in the game.

4. Once the games are complete, divide the class into groups so that students can play each other's games.

MATERIALS
<ul>
<li>1 almanac for each student</li>
<li>posterboard</li>
<li>miscellaneous supplies to create a board game, such as index cards, construction paper, markers, and glue</li>
</ul>

Almanac World Tour

STUDENT OBJECTIVE

• Extract information from an almanac using the table of contents and index.

This activity challenges students to use their map-reading skills as well as their skills in locating and extracting pertinent information from an almanac. Decorate the classroom with fact-filled slips of paper hanging from strings.

MATERIALS

• large classroom map

• 1 almanac and 1 atlas for each student or pair of students

• precut slips of paper

• string or thin ribbon

• hole punch

WHAT TO DO

1. Model this activity for students. Using a large classroom map, select a route around the world that you would like to travel. Discuss your thinking behind the route that you choose. As you select your path, record the names of the countries that you will pass through on your journey.

2. Explain that before you take this journey, you will need to learn a little more about some of the countries that you will be passing through. In order to learn more, you will use an almanac to gather some quick facts.

3. Next, demonstrate how you would use the table of contents or index to identify one of the countries that you will pass through. Once you do so, select some important information about the country. You can record the average temperatures during the summer months, the size of the country, the capital city, and so on.

4. Then, challenge students to create their own world tour. Ask them to follow the same steps that you did to select a path and to begin recording information. This activity can be done individually or in small groups.

5. After students have selected their path, recorded the countries through which they will pass, and identified those countries that they would like to learn a little more about, they should begin to gather their facts.

6. Each student or group should record each fact on a slip of paper that includes the name of the country. Once they have completed all of the countries that they selected, they should attach the papers with string or ribbon in the order which they would pass through the countries on their journey.

7. Once each group or individual has shared his tour, display the strings of countries and facts near or around a world map.

8. Challenge students to articulate why they chose the route that they did.

What If?

STUDENT OBJECTIVE

• Utilize an almanac to solve everyday questions

Posing questions that ask students to provide specific information about everyday scenarios will test their ability to navigate the almanac.

WHAT TO DO

1. Distribute the activity sheet to students. Depending upon the number of available resources, have students work individually or with a partner to answer the questions.

2. Once students have answered the questions, spend time discussing their responses. Also, discuss how well students were able to locate the necessary information and any strategies that they used to get there.

MATERIALS

• 1 almanac for each student or pair of students

• copies of the What If? sheet (page 26)

ANSWER KEY

1. euros; 2. warm-weather clothing; 3. Michael Johnson; 4. William Henry Harrison;
5. Mt. Pinatubo, El Chichon, Mt. St. Helens, Mt. Taal, Mt. Lamington; 6. Blue Ridge Parkway (most visited in 2001); 7. 2003: The Lord of the Rings: The Return of the King, 2002: Chicago, 2001: A Beautiful Mind, 2000: Gladiator; 8. Mt. McKinley

Name _____ Date _____

What If . . .?

Think about the following real-life scenarios. Put yourself in each scene. Use an almanac to answer the questions.

1. You will be taking a class trip to Italy. You will want to purchase souvenirs. What currency will you be using? _____

2. You have a friend who lives in Sydney, Australia. You are planning to visit her in December. What type of clothing should you pack for your trip?

_____

3. You are a student reporter for your local newspaper. You are asked to write a feature story about the 2000 Olympic gold medal athlete who won the 400-meter run, whom will you write about? _____

4. For a U.S. history project, you need to make coins that commemorate the first 15 presidents of the United States. You can't remember the ninth president. Who is he?

_____

5. In science you are studying volcanoes from all over the world. You need to know three different volcanoes that have erupted in the last 100 years. What are their names?

_____

6. For your summer vacation you have decided that you want to see the ten most popular national monuments in the country. You want to begin with the most popular. Which is it?

_____

7. For his birthday, your grandfather wants a new DVD for the four Academy Award-winning movies from 2000–2003. Which DVDs will you buy?

_____

_____

8. You have just taken up the sport of mountain climbing. Your goal is to climb the highest mountain in the United States someday. Which mountain will that be?

_____

Thesaurus

The Role of the Thesaurus in Your Classroom

While the thesaurus may not be the most frequently used resource in your classroom, it can be an asset when helping to enrich students' vocabulary and extend their writing. Because they can vary in their organization, providing students with a variety of texts can help to acquaint them to the purpose, style and organization of a thesaurus. As you begin to incorporate the resource into your curriculum, listen as students experiment with new words, sometimes inserting them correctly into sentences and at other times misinterpreting the meaning or word choice. In either case, students will be engaging in valuable word play that will serve to broaden their vocabulary experience.

Lessons

Synonym Search

STUDENT OBJECTIVE

• Become familiar with the organization and content of a thesaurus

Use the following activity to motivate students to identify their own synonyms and then to locate additional ones by using a thesaurus.

WHAT TO DO

1. Ask students to brainstorm a list of as many synonyms as possible for the word *big*. After a sufficient amount of time, list on the chalkboard the words elicited from students.

2. Next, ask students to use the thesaurus placed on their desks to identify more synonyms for the word *big*. Add those words to the list.

MATERIALS

- 1 thesaurus for each student or pair of students
- copies of the Seeking Synonyms sheet (page 31)

3. Discuss the role that the thesaurus played in helping to identify additional synonyms. Ask how many students found it helpful to use the resource to locate words that they may not have thought of otherwise.

4. Once students are comfortable searching for synonyms using the thesaurus, distribute copies of the activity sheet for them to complete.

Adjectives That Advertise

STUDENT OBJECTIVE

- Use a thesaurus to find synonyms to better describe a product

Using real-life materials such as magazine advertisements will engage students while they work to locate synonyms for products that have relevance in their everyday lives.

MATERIALS

- magazine advertise-ments of products that are familiar to students
- colored construction paper
- 1 thesaurus for each student or pair of students
- white drawing paper for the "new and improved" advertisements
- markers or colored pencils
- copies of the Sentences Under Construction sheet (page 32)

WHAT TO DO

1. Gather advertisements from magazines. The advertisements should be rich with adjectives.

2. Mount each ad on a piece of construction paper (laminate if possible).

3. Give each student or small group an ad and ask them to locate the adjectives that the advertiser has included in each advertisement.

4. Once you have checked that students have indeed located the appropriate words, challenge them to find synonyms for those adjectives.

5. Students should use a thesaurus to find words that could be substitutes for the adjectives found in each ad.

6. Challenge students to create new ads for the products in their advertisements. Students should incorporate the new words or synonyms found in the thesaurus.

7. Invite students to share their new ads with the class.

8. For extra practice in replacing dull adjectives, distribute copies of the activity sheet for students to complete.

Painting Pictures With Your Words

STUDENT OBJECTIVE

• Use a thesaurus to locate words that better describe a scene or action in a picture

Helping students to learn the power of words and the importance of appropriate word choice will be a valuable lesson for later writing assignments.

WHAT TO DO

1. Spend time gathering pictures from newspapers and/or magazines. The scenes should contain a lot of action or detail.

2. Mount and laminate the pictures so that they can be used again.

3. Provide each student or group with a picture. Ask them to write sentences or a brief paragraph that describes what they see in their picture.

4. Once the writing is complete, devise a way to have students trade their paragraphs and pictures.

5. After reading another's writing, challenge the students to look for places where they can add more specific, detailed words or phrases to their classmates' work.

6. Encourage students to use a thesaurus to help them find words that are more suitable and that paint a clearer mental picture of the scenes being described.

7. Students then should rewrite the sentences or paragraphs.

8. Allow students to share revised drafts with the original authors to determine if and/or how the new version paints a clearer picture of the illustration.

EXTRA! EXTRA!

As you see interesting, funny, poignant or otherwise noteworthy illustrations in magazines or newspapers, cut and laminate them. The pictures can be used repeatedly for a variety of activities.

> ## MATERIALS
>
> • 1 thesaurus for each student or group of students
>
> • photographs or pictures of action-packed scenes

Two Heads Are Better Than One—Peer Editing

STUDENT OBJECTIVE

• Edit another's work to identify places where a thesaurus could be used to find words that are more vivid

Encouraging students to share their own writing with one another, and then to use that writing to practice editing, makes the activity more authentic and valuable to the students, as well as reinforces the use of the thesaurus.

MATERIALS

• original student writing

• 1 thesaurus for each student pair or group of students

WHAT TO DO

1. Ask students to select a favorite entry from their writer's journal or portfolio of creative writing to share with a partner or small group.

2. After the entry has been read, the partner or group should help the author to identify places in the writing that could use additional details or more specific wording.

3. Once words or sentences have been identified, challenge the author to use a thesaurus to identify more specific words that can enhance the writing by making it more detailed and vivid.

4. When the entry or portion of the entry has been rewritten, have each group or pair share their newly revised writing.

5. Challenge them to determine whether or not the revision was helpful.

Name _____ Date _____

Seeking Synonyms

Look carefully at the illustration on the left. Then read the adjectives that describe the dog. Use a thesaurus to locate synonyms for each of the words. An example has been completed for you.

small _tiny_____   happy _____

playful _____   loud _____

Take a close look at the picture on the left. Think about adjectives that would describe different aspects of the items that are labeled in the picture. On each line provided, write an adjective that you think best describes the item. Then, use a thesaurus to find synonyms for each of the adjectives that you have selected.

cake _____   birthday boy _____

_____   _____

a wrapped birthday   party
present _____   decorations _____

_____   _____

Write five sentences or a brief paragraph that describes the birthday scene. In each of the sentences, include at least one of the adjectives and/or synonyms listed beside the picture to make your sentences more detailed.

_____

_____

_____

_____

_____

_____

_____

Name _____ Date _____

Sentences Under Construction

The sentences on this page are all correctly written. However, they could be more descriptive. Read each sentence and note the underlined word. Use a thesaurus to find a more descriptive synonym for that word. Rewrite the sentence using the new word.

1. Mom, your spaghetti is really <u>delicious</u>. _____
_____

2. The <u>loud</u> music really made me want to dance. _____
_____

3. When I first saw the Empire State Building, I couldn't believe how <u>big</u> it was!
_____

4. I <u>walked</u> toward the circus clown to get the balloon that he was giving away.
_____

5. John was <u>happy</u> that his family had just won the lottery. _____
_____

6. "The performance was <u>good</u>!" exclaimed the film critic. _____
_____

7. The babysitter <u>moved</u> across the room without a sound so as not to disturb the sleeping children. _____
_____

8. The policeman <u>said</u>, "Watch out! That bridge might collapse!" _____
_____

9. The <u>nice</u> crossing guard helped the children cross the crowded street. _____
_____

10. The farmer watched as the <u>small</u> animal crawled into its hole under the barn wall.
_____

Follow-up: Write your own sentence using a synonym for either <u>hot</u> or <u>cold</u>.
_____
_____
_____

Dictionary

The Role of the Dictionary in Your Classroom

First of all, it is important for students to understand that dictionaries come in many shapes and sizes and contain information that can be used for multiple purposes. While students most likely have had experiences with dictionaries in the past, many often struggle with locating the desired information efficiently. Giving them an opportunity to practice locating words and information in unique ways will help them to gain confidence using a dictionary.

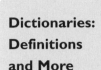

Dictionaries: Definitions and More
Besides providing definitions, the dictionary is a great resource for determining parts of speech, learning how to pronounce words, seeing the relationship between words with the same prefixes, decoding acronyms and abbreviations, and much more.

Lessons

Dictionary Discovery

STUDENT OBJECTIVES
• Become familiar with content and organization of a dictionary
• Create a definition for dictionary

Reintroducing the dictionary to students and taking the time to look at its many uses in your classroom may help to encourage students to utilize this valuable resource more often and with greater ease and efficiency.

WHAT TO DO

1. Gather as many different types of dictionaries as possible, to begin exploring and discussing the numerous aspects of a dictionary.

2. Divide students into groups and distribute several dictionaries to each group.

3. Allow students to look through the dictionaries and begin thinking about a definition for a dictionary based on what the books have in common.

MATERIALS

- multiple copies of different dictionaries for each group of students
- prompts listed on the chalkboard to guide students when exploring the dictionaries
- posterboard
- markers in various colors

4. Provide questions or prompts that will help students look for specific traits common to dictionaries. For example, you might ask students to notice:

- how the words are arranged on the page
- various fonts and boldface words
- the format of each entry
- corresponding illustrations or photographs
- guide words
- parts of the dictionary that are easy to read, eye-catching, and helpful

5. As a class, create a definition for a dictionary to add to the Information Corner.

EXTRA! EXTRA!

Once you have identified all the parts of a dictionary entry, create a large, poster-sized entry to display. Label each part of the entry in different colors so that they are easy to identify. Use it in the Information Corner as a reminder to students.

Trying Dictionaries on for Size

STUDENT OBJECTIVE

- Learn that not all dictionaries are appropriate and helpful

Often students do not have access to age-appropriate dictionaries. They may shy away from utilizing a dictionary if they have not had success using one. It is our responsibility to show them the ease and value in using a dictionary that matches their comprehension level.

WHAT TO DO

1. Once you establish reasons for using a dictionary, distribute adult-level dictionaries to groups of students.

2. Ask students to define a word that you assign. Be sure the word has a definition that they will have trouble understanding. The goal is for students to realize that not all dictionaries will be useful to them.

3. After discussing the definition and their interpretation of the definition, ask students whether they feel that the dictionary was helpful to them.

4. Now, distribute age-appropriate dictionaries to students.

5. Ask them to define a word that you assign.

6. Discuss the difference in their understanding of both definitions. Help students to realize the importance of using dictionaries that are appropriate for their reading and comprehension level.

EXTRA! EXTRA!

Often children will use dictionaries at home. When they record the definitions, it is obvious that they are not any closer to understanding the word because the definition is too difficult for them to understand. Emphasize to parents the need for their children to have home access to resources that are age-appropriate and consistent with their comprehension and reading level.

ABC Roundup

STUDENT OBJECTIVE

• Practice alphabetizing words

Being able to efficiently find words in a dictionary depends greatly on students' facility with locating words in alphabetical order. The more familiar they are with the order of the alphabet, the less likely they will become frustrated. Provide opportunities in the classroom for students to practice alphabetizing prior to asking them to locate words in a dictionary.

WHAT TO DO

1. Challenge the class to alphabetize lists of spelling words, vocabulary words within a current unit, students' names, favorite things, or any list that you and students can think of.

2. For a whole-group activity, challenge students to each come up with a word that begins with the same letter. For example, go around the room and have each student think of a word that begins with the letter B. Record all of the words on the chalkboard in random order. Then, have students alphabetize the words on a sheet of paper. This will be more difficult because the first letters will all be the same.

3. Another group activity can be to start with an "A" word such as apple or aardvark. Then go around the room as many times as you like, having the students call out words in alphabetical order. The next student may say "artichoke," then the next "balloon," then the next "cartoon"—any word will work as long as it falls after the previous letter in the

MATERIALS

• notebook paper

• pencils

• index cards with holes punched and strings through them for students to wear around their necks or wrists

• whistle or bell (optional)

alphabet. Further challenge your class by going through the alphabet backwards or by sticking with one category as they name words in alphabetical order (for example, people's names, brand names, and so on).

4. This activity provides practice in alphabetizing as well as teamwork and cooperation. Write words on index cards that are attached to strings (include some words that begin with the same letter). Invite students wear a word around their neck. Once each student is wearing a word, challenge the class to line up in alphabetical order. Challenge them to line up without saying a word. Additionally, have a student "referee" blow a whistle when a student's word is "off sides" (out of alphabetical order).

EXTRA! EXTRA!

It is always helpful to have the alphabet posted, whether it is above the chalkboard, around the perimeter of the classroom, or on students' individual desks. No matter what age, students can always benefit from having easy access to the alphabet to locate words more efficiently. In my classroom, we create our own alphabet chain. Each student is responsible for drawing and creatively coloring a letter or two from the alphabet. Each letter is drawn on 8 1/2- by 11-inch white paper. We post our letters around the classroom and display our spelling words alphabetically beneath each letter.

Having spelling words and current unit vocabulary visible encourages students to use the words frequently and to spell them correctly.

Finding Your Way Through a Dictionary

STUDENT OBJECTIVES
• Identify the use of guide words in a dictionary
• Use guide words to locate specific words

After you have completed activities that allow students to practice alphabetizing, it will be time for them to practice locating words using the guide words at the top of each dictionary page. Students are usually resistant to using the guide words and will rely on any word they may notice on a page to help them to locate their desired word. They need to practice and feel comfortable using guide words which, in turn, greatly aids them in locating words more efficiently. Students will enjoy this activity without knowing that it provides added practice in alphabetizing.

WHAT TO DO

1. Select two students to each hold a card that depicts guide words on a fictional dictionary page.

2. The two students should stand near one another in the classroom.

3. Distribute to the rest of the class cards that contain words that would and would not fall between the two guide words the students in front of the class are holding.

4. Next, ask students to study their word to determine whether or not it would fit between the guide words.

5. If a student believes his or her word would fall between the two, then he or she should walk to the front of the room and stand between the two students.

6. If the word does not fit, the student should walk to the opposite end of the room. When all of the students have gotten into place, go around the room and have each student read his or her word so that the others can check the accuracy of their classmates.

7. Create an additional challenge by asking students to place themselves in alphabetical order between the two students who are holding the guide words.

MATERIALS
• sheets of large cardstock paper (for guide words)
• sheets of small cardstock paper (for entry words)
• markers

EXTRA! EXTRA!
Challenging students to race to find a word can illustrate the value in using guide words to help them identify words more efficiently.

1. If you have a large quantity of dictionaries that are the same, hand them out so that every two students can share a dictionary.

2. Call out a word.

3. Encourage students to thumb through the dictionary until they find the word or the page where they think the word would fall.

4. When a team has found the page, they can call out "Found it!" and share the page number.

5. Don't move on until everyone locates the desired page and finds the word.

6. The winning team is the one that called out "Found it!" (correctly) most often.

Take a Closer Look

STUDENT OBJECTIVE
• Identify parts of a dictionary entry

Dictionary entries can be confusing and difficult to decipher when students are unfamiliar with their content. Students need to understand that dictionary entries contain much more than just the definition of a word. Before expecting students to access information from a dictionary entry, help them to understand its various aspects and their uses in our daily language.

MATERIALS
• posterboard

• markers

• copies of a sample entry from a children's dictionary

• copies of the Dictionary Dig sheet (page 42)

WHAT TO DO

1. On a large piece of posterboard, recreate an entry that contains examples of all of its possible parts. Be sure to color-code the different parts of the entry.

2. Also, recreate the same entry on paper to distribute to students.

3. In groups or individually, ask students to label each part of the entry based on their own interpretation of what is there.

4. Then, explore the entry with students. Ask them to identify and name the various parts and provide reasons for including them in an entry. During your discussion, label the large poster-size entry.

5. Place the poster in your Information Corner.

6. For extra practice with the various aspects of dictionary entries, distribute copies of the activity sheet for students to complete.

Which Meaning?

STUDENT OBJECTIVE

• Choose the correct definition from an entry with multiple definitions

Students need to understand that some words have multiple definitions. In these cases, they must identify and choose the definition that best suits the word in a particular context. It is helpful to illustrate this by using familiar words.

WHAT TO DO

1. Write the two sentences on the chalkboard:

> He stood in <u>line</u> for an hour to get the race car driver's autograph.
>
> The actor did not remember his <u>lines</u> in time for the performance.

2. Now, ask the students what is similar about both sentences. They should remark that both sentences contain the word <u>line</u>.

3. Next, have them identify that each sentence uses the word <u>line</u> differently.

4. Ask students to look up the word <u>line</u> in the dictionary. Have them identify the correct definition for each sentence according to the context clues provided.

5. Before moving on, ask the students whether there are other definitions listed for the word <u>line</u>.

6. Create an extra challenge by asking students to brainstorm other words that have multiple meanings. They can create sentences to illustrate their difference in meaning or create illustrations to depict the difference visually.

> **MATERIALS**
> • 1 dictionary for each pair of students or small group
> • copies of the Which Meaning? sheet (page 44)

Sorting Game

STUDENT OBJECTIVE
• Utilize word-locating skills

Another way students can use their word-locating skills in a dictionary, as well as recognize the parts of a word entry, is to play Word Sort. This activity challenges both their critical-thinking and dictionary skills.

MATERIALS
• 1 dictionary for each pair of students or small group
• notebook paper

WHAT TO DO

1. Provide students with a list of words that are in some way related. Ask students to identify and categorize the words according to their similarities.

2. Ask students to first define and then sort the following words by definition. Remind students to label each category.

- carburetor
- transmission
- appendix
- axle
- engine
- muscle
- artery
- bicuspid

3. Ask students look up each of the following words to determine its part of speech. Then students should sort the words, and create and label the categories.

- unruly
- patriotic
- flinch
- occupation
- indent
- linger
- pavement
- spacious

4. Challenge students to come up with their own Word Sort games based on current units of study or topics of interest.

Create-a-Dictionary

STUDENT OBJECTIVE

• Combine learned information about a dictionary to create one's own dictionary

Students can use their knowledge of dictionaries to create a dictionary that will meet their own needs. For example, if students are working on a solar-system unit, they can create a dictionary that includes the new vocabulary words that they acquire. In fact, creating a dictionary throughout the unit is a helpful study tool to reinforce important literacy skills such as parts of speech, word usage, and so on. Challenging students to create a dictionary at the end of a unit is a legitimate way to assess their knowledge and understanding of the material covered. Maintaining a personal dictionary serves as a reminder to use their newly acquired vocabulary.

WHAT TO DO

1. Use the template to create a model to show students how to make their own personal dictionaries.

2. Distribute several blank copies of the template to each student so that they can create a page each time they want to add a word to their dictionary.

3. Encourage students to use a folder or binder to keep the pages organized in alphabetical order for easy access and use.

MATERIALS

• copies of the Create-a-Dictionary template (page 43)

• 1 pocket folder or three-ring binder for each student

Name _____ Date _____

Dictionary Dig

Like archaeologists digging up pieces of our ancient past, you can learn more about dictionaries and what they contain by exploring with a Dictionary Dig.

1. Find a five-syllable word. _____

2. Find a noun. _____

3. Find a word entry that contains a suffix or a prefix for the entry word. _____

4. Find a word with multiple definitions. _____

5. Find a two-syllable word. _____

6. Find an adjective. _____

7. Find a word with a long-vowel sound. _____

8. Find a word that begins with a C that is a noun. _____

9. Find a word that begins with a P that has two syllables. _____

10. Find a verb. _____

11. Find a word that can be made plural. _____

12. Find a set of guide words that begin with X. _____

13. Find a two-letter word. _____

14. Write the phonetic spelling of _____. _____

15. Find a word that has an illustration beside it. _____

Name _____ Date _____

Create-a-Dictionary

Word: _____

Definition(s): _____

_____

Part of speech:

_____

Sentence that includes the word: _____

_____

_____

_____

Illustration that describes the word:

Name _____ Date _____

Which Meaning?

Read each pair of sentences. Use a dictionary to identify the definition of the underlined word. Below each sentence, write the correct definition for the underlined word.

1. The students walked out of the classroom complaining that the test was too <u>hard</u>.

_____

He left his bubblegum on his bedpost and it became <u>hard</u> overnight.

_____

2. The <u>light</u> snow covered the roads but did not make driving difficult.

_____

With no <u>light</u> in the room, he couldn't see a thing as he searched for the doorknob.

_____

3. He decided to give the puppy a bath in the kitchen <u>sink</u>.

_____

She threw the pebble into the clear lake and watched it slowly <u>sink</u> toward the bottom.

_____

4. He couldn't find the phone number that he had written on a tiny <u>slip</u> of paper.

_____

He hurried and shoveled the sidewalk so that no one would <u>slip</u> on the slick surface.

_____

The captain sailed the boat into its <u>slip</u> at the marina.

_____

Encyclopedia

The Role of the Encyclopedia in Your Classroom

While the Internet and electronic encyclopedia have become alluring means for quickly acquiring information, the classic set of encyclopedias can still have a role in your classroom. It is important to remember that students may not always have access to technology. In those instances, they need to know how to locate information from more traditional resources. In doing so, they will realize the potential that encyclopedias possess for answering their research questions and extending their learning.

Lessons

Exploring Encyclopedias

STUDENT OBJECTIVES

- Become familiar with the contents and organization of an encyclopedia
- Define encyclopedia

Depending on students' ages, the types of resources available to them, and the nature of their research opportunities, some students may not have had access to or experience with encyclopedias. Taking the time to explore, discuss, and think about an encyclopedia will give students an advantage before they begin their next research activity.

WHAT TO DO

1. If you have a class set of encyclopedias, pass out one volume to each student.

2. As a class, explore its format, layout, and contents. As you explore, begin a discussion that leads students through

Tip!

Encyclopedias: Making Connections

Using current topics of study to introduce the encyclopedia in your classroom is the most beneficial and practical for students. However, if your current topic of study does not lend itself to the use of an encyclopedia, the ideas in this section will challenge students to familiarize themselves with the resource and utilize the information that it holds.

MATERIALS

- 1 encyclopedia volume for each pair or small group of students

the encyclopedia, extends their thinking, and familiarizes them with the resource. Possible questions include:

- *How is the encyclopedia organized?* (alphabetical order, with guide words, like an outline)
- *What might be the quickest and easiest way to locate information in an encyclopedia?* (guide words and index)
- *What type of information does an encyclopedia contain?* (information about people, places, and things)
- *How is the information organized within each topic?* (boldface words and titles, outline form)
- *Why do you think an encyclopedia is organized the way it is?* (easy to read and locate specific information that you are looking for)
- *What other resource does an encyclopedia remind you of and why?* (dictionary, because of its alphabetical order and guide words)

3. Once you have discussed the contents and organization of the encyclopedia, create a class definition for encyclopedia to place in the Information Corner.

EXTRA! EXTRA!

If students have access to an electronic encyclopedia, invite them to compare the differences (if any) in the type of information that is available, the newness of the information available, and the ease or difficulty in navigating each resource.

Classroom Zoo From A to Z

STUDENT OBJECTIVE

- Locate specific information from an encyclopedia

Provide students with an opportunity to create their own encyclopedia for use as one of your classroom resources. Animals are an easy and often intriguing topic for students. Most animal entries are filled with information that students can comprehend. If other areas of your curriculum have covered the animal world, challenge students to think of another topic for the classroom encyclopedia.

WHAT TO DO

1. Provide each student with one volume of an encyclopedia from your class set, and assign them letters.

2. Challenge each student to locate an animal in the volume. (Each volume should have an animal.)

3. This process may take a while. Those students who cannot think of an animal beginning with their assigned letter may have to leaf through the entire volume to locate one.

4. Once each student has selected an animal, ask him or her to read about the particular animal, noting the headings, boldface titles, and so on.

5. Next, there are several variations this activity can take, as in the following examples:

ACTIVITY 1: Challenge students to create an acrostic poem using the animal's name as the base of the poem, as well as using specific details and facts gathered from their reading of the encyclopedia article.

Sample Acrostic:

Lives on the African plains

If a lioness has babies, she usually has 2 or 3 in her litter.

On a male lion's back is something called a mane.

Nighttime is usually when lions hunt so that they can surprise their prey.

ACTIVITY 2: Select a particular theme for this project. For example, ask each student to find and write about a chosen animal's habitat, food, or physical characteristics and features. Once topics are identified, each student is responsible for locating specific information and compiling it into paragraph, outline, or picture form.

6. Once the research and written aspect of the assignment are complete, students can create an illustration of their animal, including all of the details that they learned.

7. Combine all of the animals in alphabetical order to create a book to include in your own classroom library.

EXTRA! EXTRA!

Challenge students to create their own encyclopedia on any number of topics such as famous faces, American historical sites, unique inventions, favorite children's authors, and so on. While they may use resources other than the encyclopedia to locate information about the selected topic, they can still compile it into an "Encyclopedia of . . ."

Details, Details, Details

STUDENT OBJECTIVE

• Enhance the information displayed throughout the classroom by locating additional details to support it

One way to use an encyclopedia to extend your curriculum is to utilize the art, words, and work already present in your classroom.

MATERIALS

• various encyclopedias

• white drawing paper

• thin markers

WHAT TO DO

1. Challenge students to look around the room to identify one poster, sign, bulletin board display, or notice that they would like to research. For example, in my classroom is a poster of a haiku written by Buson. One of my students might research the author or haiku poems in general. Another student might research facts about France to place around the photographs of France that are hanging on the wall in my classroom.

2. Once the information has been written in some form, post the facts near or around the corresponding display.

Independent Research

STUDENT OBJECTIVES

• Identify a topic of interest to research
• Use an encyclopedia to access information on a specific topic

Often our students are assigned activities and projects that have no relevance to their daily lives or are of little interest to them. Provide students with opportunities to research topics that truly interest or fascinate them. If you do so, you will find a motivated student who is eager to begin a thorough investigation.

WHAT TO DO

1. Early in the year, ask students to begin a list of topics that they would like to learn more about. This as an ongoing independent research list students keep in their file or portfolio so that they can add to it as interest arises. It is important to allow students to create a list without our influence or suggestion. (Initially, they may want examples of topics such as "poisonous snakes in our region" or "Why do volcanoes erupt?")

2. Designate time in your day or week to allow students to begin researching a topic from their list. Prior to initiating research, distribute copies of the activity sheet so that students can plan their course of action.

3. Once they establish a plan, encourage students to begin their research using an encyclopedia as their first resource. The amount of information available in an encyclopedia will dictate whether they need to extend their search into other resources.

4. As students begin to navigate the encyclopedia, encourage them to think about the different key words that they may look up. For example, if students are researching why volcanoes erupt, they will probably look up "volcano" first. Then, they may look up a specific volcano. After that, they may look up a related topic listed at the end of the encyclopedia entry. Encourage them to exhaust every possibility before electing to move on to another resource.

5. Once students have completed the predetermined requirements for the research and have sufficiently documented their newfound information, invite them to think of a unique way to display or demonstrate their knowledge on the topic.

6. Students may choose to present their newly acquired information visually, orally, or in written form. Whichever way they choose to relay their information, provide opportunities for students to share their research.

Name _____ Date _____

Independent Research Planning Guide

My topic is: _____

The questions that I want to answer are: _____

_____

_____

_____

_____

_____

I will get my information from the following resources: _____

_____

_____

_____

_____

My final project will be: _____

_____

_____

_____

_____

_____

_____

The Internet

The Role of the Internet in Your Classroom

One of the most recent and popular research resources is the Internet. It is a tool that holds much lure and wonder because of its amazing capabilities. Incorporating into your curriculum activities and lessons that encourage students to utilize the Internet for gathering information will certainly help them familiarize themselves with the research tool and all that it has to offer. The wonderful thing about the Internet is the opportunity that it affords both teachers and their students to learn from one another.

Demonstrating how to navigate through sites and links within the Internet will arm students with the tools necessary to access unique information. Guiding them through kid-friendly sites and monitoring their use are our responsibilities. Please preview each site to be sure the material is suitable for the developmental level of your students. Consider bookmarking sites as a way to lead students directly to the pages you want them to view.

Valuable Information

One of the benefits of incorporating the Internet into students' research repertoire is that they can easily read up-to-the-minute information. However, it's a good idea to encourage students to read Web information with a degree of skepticism. Though a wealth of interesting and educational information is on the Internet, help students determine which sites might be more reliable and which might not be a good source to reference.

Lessons

What Else Is There?

STUDENT OBJECTIVE

- Learn the value of the Internet as a resource tool by extending or enhancing a current research project

Assign this activity after students have completed some research or projects without the benefit of the Internet as a reference tool.

WHAT TO DO

1. Ask students to select a piece of research from their portfolio.

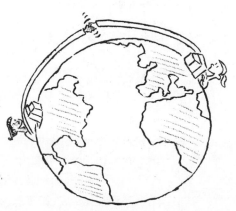

2. Using a quality, child-friendly search engine (see examples of sites below), challenge students to conduct a topic search to find additional information. The purpose of the activity is to help them discover the breadth and depth of the information available on the Internet and to compare that information with the type of information available to them from other, more traditional research sources.

3. Once students have gathered enough information to extend their previous research, initiate a conversation comparing reference tools. Use the following questions to guide your discussion.

- *Which resource gave you more information?*
- *Which resource gave you better information?*
- *How was the information from the various sources different?*
- *How was the information from the various sources similar?*

Examples of kid-friendly sites:

Yahooligans!   www.yahooligans.com

OneKey   www.onekey.com

Ask Jeeves Kids   www.ajkids.com

EXTRA! EXTRA!

Inform students that when they are conducting a topic search, quotation marks can be very important to the whole process. For example, if you enter your search topic without quotation marks around it, the search will yield sites and information about anything related to all of the words that you listed in the search box. If you place quotation marks around the words in the search box, the search will yield sites related to the exact words that you placed within the marks.

"I Wonder . . ." Internet Question of the Day

STUDENT OBJECTIVE

- Explore the Internet using kid-friendly sites to locate answers to specific questions

To help students understand the many opportunities for gathering an array of information try an Internet Question of the Day. The purpose of the activity is twofold. First, it will give students further guidance as you model how to weed through Web sites in order to locate one that will answer a specific question or address a specific purpose. Secondly, it will serve to increase exposure to different sites on a variety of topics.

WHAT TO DO

1. Place a question box prominently in your classroom.

2. Encourage students to submit to the box questions about topics of interest to them. The topics can relate to current topics of study or any student interest or hobby.

3. Gather the class and have them watch as you model asking the question and then exploring the Internet to answer it. If available, use a large screen monitor for easier viewing for the whole group.

4. As you select questions and locate answers, you will no doubt stumble upon valuable Web sites. Keep a running list of useful, fascinating, worthy-of-another-look Web sites near the computer. During free time, students can access sites from the list to explore a topic further.

MATERIALS
- decorated "question" box
- computers with access to the Internet (large screen monitor, if available)

Web Address Book

STUDENT OBJECTIVES
- Become familiar with an interesting Web site to share with the class
- Begin an ongoing list of favorite Web sites

Encouraging students to share an age-appropriate site of their choosing will be an exciting task. It will allow students to demonstrate their facility with a site as well as their interest behind selecting it. No doubt, the class will be introduced to an array of fun, fascinating, silly and even useful sites. Teachers may want to reserve the right to pre-approve each site before the presentations are prepared.

WHAT TO DO

1. Ask students to select a Web site that is a favorite or is useful to them in some way.

2. Provide time for each student to create a presentation about a Web site of their choosing. If possible, students should use a large viewing screen so that they can demonstrate the site and all that it has to offer. In the demonstration, students should include why they selected the particular site, what information it offers, and the various capabilities of the site.

3. After the presentations, encourage students to keep their own list of favorite sites. They can begin by including ones mentioned in their peers' presentations. They can use a notebook or journal, documenting the Web address and describing the content of the site.

MATERIALS
- computers with access to the Internet (large screen monitor, if available)

Reading Wish List

STUDENT OBJECTIVES

• Use appropriate Web sites to identify children's book reviews
• Create a reading "wish list"

Using the Internet to read book reviews and gather information about books is a great opportunity for students. Combining students' love of reading with their desire to "surf" the Web will prove fruitful in helping students to develop a "wish list" of books for future reading.

MATERIALS

• computers with access to the Internet

• copies of the Reading Wish List sheet (page 56)

• 1 pocket folder for each student

WHAT TO DO

1. Begin the activity by asking students how they select books to read. Some may answer that they use their friends' recommendations, the librarian's book talks, or book reviews in student book orders and/or children's periodicals.

2. Provide students with sites that review books and conduct chats with or provide information about favorite children's authors.

3. Students need time to browse for books using the sites that you have identified or ones that they have located on their own.

4. Once they have identified books that interest them, ask students to record those books on their "wish list" sheet.

5. Encourage students to refer to the wish lists whenever they visit the library. Remind them that the lists can be ongoing, and to check off a book after they have read it.

EXTRA! EXTRA!

Because students trust their peers and often enjoy similar genres and books, encourage them to share those books that they particularly enjoyed. Once students finish books that they found via an Internet book review, invite them to write their own review of the book. Student reviews can be posted or filed in the classroom to encourage others to read the books as well.

In the News

STUDENT OBJECTIVES
- Increase awareness of current news events
- Locate and use a children's news Web site to identify a current news event

Depending upon your classroom structure and daily routine, create a time when a student can share a current news event with the class. This can be done daily during your morning meeting or as an end-of-week wrap-up.

WHAT TO DO

MATERIALS
- computers with access to the Internet

1. Create a schedule that assigns each student a time to locate a current news event to present to the class.

2. When his or her designated day or week arrives, provide sufficient time for each student to access a set list of Web sites in order to identify a newsworthy event to share with the class.

3. Encourage students to orally summarize the event, complete with all pertinent details. Students may choose to update stories that have been previously introduced, find news of local, state, and national interest, or identify news stories that relate to topics being discussed in the classroom.

4. After the news event has been presented, allow time for questions and/or a discussion.

EXTRA! EXTRA!
Keep a list of helpful kid-friendly Web sites near the computer for easy access. A clipboard or an index card box is an easy way to organize and store frequently used Web site addresses near the computer. Also, encourage students to include those sites in their own Web address book.

Name _____ Date _____

Reading Wish List

Title: _____

Author: _____

Genre: _____

What's the book about? _____

_____

Title: _____

Author: _____

Genre: _____

What's the book about? _____

_____

Title: _____

Author: _____

Genre: _____

What's the book about? _____

_____

Title: _____

Author: _____

Genre: _____

What's the book about? _____

_____

Title: _____

Author: _____

Genre: _____

What's the book about? _____

_____

Putting It All Together

The ABC's of a Country

STUDENT OBJECTIVE

• Access information from a variety of resources to identify facts about a specific country

Once students are familiar with a variety of learning resources, they can begin to practice locating specific information contained in them. One way to get students to use all of the skills they've learned is to challenge them to create an alphabet book about a specific topic. For example, students can create an ABC book about a country. Challenge them to utilize all the resources discussed in this workbook to access information to produce a book that alphabetically informs its readers about a country.

For example, for the letter P, a student can record a country's population. For the letter R a student can identify how much rain falls in a particular portion of the country that they are studying. For the letter T, the student can write about the type of import and export trade the country does. Encourage the students to be creative when thinking about the type of information to include with each letter of the alphabet.

Napoleon **B**onaparte was Emperor of France from 1804 to 1814.

The **A**lps are mountains that create a border between France and Italy.

There are many **C**astles in the Loire River Valley.

MATERIALS

- a variety of reference resources (atlas, almanac, encyclopedia, Internet)

- copies of the planning sheets (pages 59–64)

- white 8 1/2- by 11-inch paper

- white cardstock paper for book cover

- markers and colored pencils

WHAT TO DO

1. Students must select a country or one can be assigned to them.

2. Use the brainstorm sheets to think of possible topics to research based on each letter of the alphabet. This can be done individually by each student and then discussed as a whole class. The topics that you discuss then can be written on poster board and displayed for everyone as they collect information about their country.

3. Provide students with the ABC data collection sheets. This is where the students will record the information that relates to each letter of the alphabet. It is helpful to encourage students to keep the data collection sheets organized in a folder or binder.

4. Once the facts have been gathered for each letter, the information then needs to be written in well-constructed sentences.

5. Use whatever editing process students are familiar with to edit each of their letter pages.

6. Each student will then need to type or write each letter-related fact onto a clean piece of white 8 1/2- by 11-inch paper. Keep in mind that each letter will be represented on one page. Therefore, each student will have to record information on 26 pages. Remind students to write their information on either the bottom or top of each page so that there is sufficient room for a detailed illustration.

7. Once each page has been completed in final draft form, students should create an illustration on that page that relates to the information being described in the sentence(s).

8. Ask each student to create a colorful cover for his or her ABC book.

9. When complete, the book pages can be bound in alphabetical order and then displayed in the classroom for others to read.

Name _____ Date _____

ABC's of a Country—Topic Search

On the lines provided, write ideas of possible topics that relate to each of the letters of the alphabet. For example, on line *P* you could write *population*, *products*, or the name of a city or river that exists in your country that begins with the letter P. For S you could write size, national song, sports, etc.

Be creative!
Try to think of topics and subjects that will allow your readers to really learn about the country you are researching.

A _____

_____

B _____

_____

C _____

_____

D _____

_____

E _____

_____

F _____

_____

G _____

_____

H _____

_____

I _____

_____

J _____

_____

K _____

_____

L _____

_____

M _____

_____

N _____

_____

O _____

_____

P _____

_____

Q _____

_____

R _____

_____

S _____

_____

T _____

_____

U _____

_____

V _____

_____

W _____

_____

X _____

_____

Y _____

_____

Z _____

_____

Name _____ Date _____

ABC's of a Country—Data Collection Sheet

On the lines provided, write the facts and information that relate to each letter and topic that you have selected.

A _____

_____ Source: _____

B _____

_____ Source: _____

C _____

_____ Source: _____

D _____

_____ Source: _____

E _____

_____ Source: _____

F _____

_____ Source: _____

G _____

_____ Source: _____

H _____

_____ Source: _____

I _____

_____ Source: _____

J _____

_____ Source: _____

K _____

_____ Source: _____

L _____

_____ Source: _____

M _____

_____ Source: _____

N _____

_____ Source: _____

O _____

_____ Source: _____

P _____

_____ Source: _____

Q _____

_____ Source: _____

R _____

_____ Source: _____

S _____

_____ Source: _____

T _____

_____ Source: _____

U _____

_____ Source: _____

V _____

_____ Source: _____

W _____

_____ Source: _____

X _____

_____ Source: _____

Y _____

_____ Source: _____

Z _____

_____ Source: _____

Name _____ Date _____

ABC's of a Country—Draft

On the lines provided, rewrite, in compete sentences, the information that you gathered on your data collection sheets. Check for correct spelling, especially those words that describe places and things related to your particular country.

A _____

_____

B _____

_____

C _____

_____

D _____

_____

E _____

_____

F _____

_____

G _____

_____

H _____

_____

I _____

_____

J _____

_____

K _____

_____

L _____

_____

M _____

_____

N _____

_____

O _____

_____

P _____

_____

Q _____

_____

R _____

_____

S _____

_____

T _____

_____

U _____

_____

V _____

_____

W _____

_____

X _____

_____

Y _____

_____

Z _____

_____